Borzellino Familia Ltd
SanDiego, California
866-458-4514.
6965 El Camino Real
#105-560
Carlsbad, California 92009

DIGIT

7

PERSPECTIVES

How to double your income using higher level thinking

By John Borzellino

Thank you

As always, I thank my Heavenly Father for all my blessings

To my wife Sharon, for your energy, your love and your angelic smile

To my children Audrey, Hannah, Evan and Sophia
and for their spirits and singing

To my mentors for teaching me

To my clients for believing in me

And to every second I am alive for including me

Library of Congress Cataloging in Publication Data

Borzellino, John.
Digit 7 Perspectives

Printed in the United States of America

John Borzellino and Digit 7 Perspectives

"In my 30 years of journalism, I have not known anyone who connects with people, to bring about change, like John Borzellino. John built his systems into an intricate science and art that can be the basis of a highly profitable enterprise. He is a business visionary, a self-made millionaire, a modern-day mentor and a catalyst for change."
—John Cunniff, Head Business Writer, Associated Press

"You have a very innovative and thoughtful program of education."
—Milton Mitler, Vice President, Special Assistant to the President, Chamber of Commerce of the United States of America, Washington DC

"Your insights are indeed brilliant. I look forward to reading your upcoming Digit 7 Perspectives book."
—Gansha Pon to John Borzellino at the 8th World Congress at New York University, August 3, 2003 after hearing John's Change Philosophy presentation.

"John can help you move up to a whole new six-figure you . . . John Borzellino is all about cluing people into a way to do a lot better than they've ever done before."
—Gerald Bendix, *San Francisco Chronicle*

"His flamboyant style, his furious ambition have helped him use the lessons he's learned to make millions."
—Richard Poe, Senior Editor, *Success Magazine* / Great Comebacks Award Winner

"His energy is infectious, his optimism endless."
—John L. Smith, *Las Vegas Review Journal*

"Congratulations on being nominated for the President's Service Award. Your outstanding volunteer service benefits the Nation. Contributions like yours are crucial to our ability to solve our country's most critical problems. On behalf of the American people, thank you for your commitment and dedication."
—President Bill Clinton / President's Service Award Winner

"It is my pleasure to commend you for your commitment. You have my best wishes for continued success."
—Governor Zell Miller

"I have no reservation in making any recommendation for John's endeavors."
—Fred Stock, Warden, United States Department of Justice, Federal Bureau of Prisons, USP Atlanta/ Honorary Warden Citation

"I am most impressed with your program. You have already taken the most appropriate steps in designing a program aimed at turning lives around."
—Senator Sam Nunn, United States Senate, Committee on Armed Services, Washington DC

"I applaud you for the work that you're doing."
—Newt Gingrich, Speaker of the House, Congress of the United States

"John's program has engendered a sense of hope among our guys that is really phenomenal."
—Eldson McGhee, President, Vietnam Veterans of America Organizing Committee

"With your business savvy, and dedicated community service, it's not surprising that your peers have honored you with this well-deserved recognition."
—Carol Harter, President, UNLV/Top 40 Under 40 Business Leader Award

"Surely your development program will be well received."
—B. Eugene Griessman, Director, Communication and Development, Georgia Institute of Technology

"We are pleased to be a collaborative partner with you."
—John Smith, Moorehouse School of Medicine

"I have looked through your materials and I am impressed. I commend you for your work."
—Gerald Bartels, President, Atlanta Chamber of Commerce

"It is an outstanding book and I am very impressed."
—James Seastrand, Mayor, City of North Las Vegas

"Thank you for helping our perspectives. Your program causes instant, dramatic thinking elevations."
—Javier Guitierez, President, Oasis Group, Cancun

"John, your thinking is pure genius. We have made immediate changes that will have long-lasting positive effects in our company."
—Emilio Huhn, President, Camino Real

"Everyone found something different as a benefit from your program. All our attendees including myself have gained a useful aid that we have continued to apply daily. I personally found your style refreshing."
—Brien Steven Pidgeon, President, Lawyers Title

"Corporations of all sizes as well as individuals will greatly improve their quality of life and productivity if they even apply only a few of your examples and perspectives."
—Jeffrey Nolan, President, Southwest Region, Corporate Banking, Nations Bank

DIGIT 7 PERSPECTIVES

SECTION TITLES

“The most powerful force
in existence is compounding.”
Albert Einstein

I
The Introduction

This book was not written to sell, it was written to connect our perspectives. For if we are able to find a commonality in our thinking, our reasoning, our philosophies, and psychologies, the manner in which we justify, rationalize and perform, we will then be in a position to double your highest net income as our first goal.

This book was written to help me find the exception. The person who is abnormal, unique, crazy, the top 1%, the person who knows they have only just begun, and have only touched the surface of their income earning potential. The person who already possesses intellectual capital in who they are, but they have been spending their time getting paid for what they do instead of getting paid for who they are.

Seven figure thinking, not six, is key. To have the mindset of the highest levels of income. To embrace the perspectives prior to the income manifesting itself, requires a psychic change. And, an acceptance of the value of *Digit 7 Perspectives.*

Money can be made in any business. It's being done every day, but typically by others. *Digit 7's* sole purpose is to determine if you feel you can learn from John Ross. Read the perspectives in this book. See if they ring true in your mind.

If they do, the goal of doubling your highest net income becomes reachable and possible. Getting out of the way is vital. It's the previous thinking that one must change in order to make dramatic income jumps. When was the last time your net income doubled?

Compression and compounding are keys. If someone makes $200,000 a year, he or she knows how to make a million, it just takes them five years to realize it. With compression of time and the compounding of effort, it can be done in one year. It requires not just new thinking, but multi-dimensional thinking.

For the next several pages, open your mind, get to a place where you will not be interrupted. Put your feet up on a chair with a nice cold drink. Relax. Take a mini-retreat from your normal mindset and chaos to see if what you read is potentially an understanding that could make a difference. If so, and you feel you have learned a remarkably fresh way to look at things, let's get together and talk.

"Everything that can be invented, has been invented."

Charles Duell, Commissioner,
United States Office of Patents, 1899

II
Outside the Coffin

Sometimes what it takes is not just thinking outside of the box, but jumping out of your own skin. Have you ever gone sky diving? You need to. Schedule your first tandem jump now. Most people feel it is dangerous. However, mortality odds are one in 50,000 compared to one in 7,000 for motor vehicular deaths. Most people drive every day without thinking about the risk. One in 400 die from heart disease and one in 600 from cancer – both are from illnesses, not accidents. And, many times these are within our control by modifying our diet, exercise and reducing or eliminating stress.

Is it fear that stops most people? Fear of what, the odds are dramatically on your side. It's much safer than driving your car. Is it the fear of falling? If so, when you jump out of a plane, there is no frame of reference. Nothing to judge how fast or how far you are falling. You actually experience a flying or floating sensation, not one of falling. You owe it to yourself to at least do it once. But don't wait.

As Tim McGraw says so eloquently in his "Live like you were dyin" CD, "I hope you get the chance to live like you were dyin'. He went sky divin', rocky mountain climbing ... he loved deeper and spoke sweeter and gave forgiveness he'd been denying."

The beauty of real estate is the possibility every day to make in one deal, your previous years income. That should be enough to keep you up late at night and get you up early in the morning with a sweet grin on your face.

But, it requires energy, new energy. Energy to change from who you are to who you want to be. You must do something dramatic. Not just a hairstyle change or moving, but more along the lines of singing in church, skiing the Alps, traveling to your grandparents birthplace or skydiving. Doing something that you always wished you would do, wanted to do, and know you need to do before there is no time left.

It's almost like those activities open the door to a whole new world. A world of high net income. A world of freedom. When will you have more time than you do right now? Not everyone has 50 more years to figure it out!

"604k ought to be enough for anybody."
Bill Gates, 1981

III
Get Me Out of My Way

The wrong thinking is dangerous to our health – it compresses our life, thus shortening it. Stress is most often caused by the wrong thinking. Most problems are disguised challenges. They are opportunities to change. Our goal needs to be an extension, an expansion of our lives. Joy, happiness, satisfaction, and contentment are words most people find only in dictionaries.

There are always excuses – "I'm too busy." What most mean is 'I'm so busy, but I'm broke." And, it's not always financially, because freedom is much more valuable than wealth. For without freedom, wealth is unattainable. The ability to do what you want, when you want. Total control over your time, now that is beautiful.

It's amazing how many people are the root of their own problems, especially men. The testosterone, male macho, 'I know what I am doing' mentality. Are you making high six or seven figures yet? If not, get out of your own way, tear up your ego and stop comparing yourself to your high school or college buddies. Realize you haven't even made any real money yet. Nothing compared to what is available and what your destiny may be.

You may even be in the top 1% earning high six-figures. But you may also be destined to earn that amount monthly, or even weekly. It's attainable. I met with the owner of one of Fortune's fastest growing privately held companies after being introduced by an investor-client of mine. The owner asked why his company needed my perspectives since his company was growing at 25% per year. I simply said "What makes you think you can't do +25% per month?"

You see his sales people were only averaging $40,000 per year. My premise was to skip the executives and teach the sales staff how to change their thinking and double their incomes. The owner felt he needed no help, even though the turnover of his sales staff was frightening. He just needed to get out of his own way and instead of making money accidentally, let all the forces work together which means allowing new thinking to enter into his formula.

Charles Barkley, from his book *I may be wrong, but I doubt it*, said "Moses Malone told me, You can come in here every day and work your ass off and still not make it. But I can guarantee you if you come in here and don't work, you won't make it. You have to be obsessed to get to the NBA finals. But what you see often in team sports

"To survive and succeed,
every organization
will have to turn itself into
a change agent.
The most effective way to
manage change
successfully is to create it."

Peter Drucker

is that after you win once or get to the championship series, guys start saying, 'I need more minutes than him,' or 'I should be making more money than that guy,' and when that's the case, you ain't gonna win. No team that is in contract disputes or major renegotiations has ever won a championship."

The trouble with young players in minor leagues, is too many of them focus on what they will do with their millions as opposed to working on their game and their attitudes to become an integral, irreplaceable part of a winning team. Winning is attitude, not talent, but professional sports has made it tough for players to remember that.

The ego, testosterone, the male machoness are obstacles in the average male's life. It gets in the way prior to even beginning communication. Like a bad smell or taste. Its difficult to deal with and all you want to do is get away from it. Remember, conceit is the disease that makes everyone sick but the person that has it. The more abundant it is, the higher the degree of natural repelent we feel. And the corporate owner felt he needed nothing, no help. He was thinking of himself, not of his staff.

Many of the people I consult with have trouble getting out of their own way. It begins with not admitting that one's current beliefs are what is keeping one mediocre. It is very difficult to admit that we need to change in order to reach our goals. Staying where you are at in life is quite comfortable for the average person.

From a scientific standpoint, one must disturb a system that is in equilibrium by either adding more reactants or removing some product in order to get the reaction to move forward again. As individuals we can get out of our own way by adding new perspective to our lives, or by removing negative thoughts or by changing a negative environment.

When a hitter gets in a slump, he is overanalyzing his swing. Analysis leads to paralysis, which doesn't work in the batters box or anywhere.

A persons disbelief in themselves enters the room prior to opening a conversation. A guy who wants to talk to a girl at a club says to himself, 'She doesn't want to talk to me. She wouldn't be interested in me'. Because, he isn't interested in himself. Our self doubts, self esteems, and self talk is what preempts the opening line or opening opportunity. We need to get out of our own way.

"Only those who dare to fail greatly can ever achieve greatly."

Robert F. Kennedy

The job of an actor is not to gain public recognition, but to convey meaning to the audience. To allow the audience to live the play. An actor needs to bring neutrality to the scene. Neutrality in who the actor is outside of the scene in real life. Their presence must be neutralized by the part they play and it is the part that becomes paramount.

Deals are like this. Emotions get in the way and people lose substantial dollars because of attitutudes, "principles", and egos.

Actors often complain about auditions, saying they are beneath them. However, the audition is the real performance, or the chance to give one, not the movie job they hope to get. Every time they audition in front of a producer, a director, or a casting agent, they are performing. Not just for that potential job or role, but for any role the Hollywood players may need them for in the future. Short-term thinking is a killer.

Most Americans want what they want and they want it now. This is a major reason why so many are overweight, maxed out on their credit cards, and working a dead-end job. Long-term thinking is the change that is vital.

Only 71 of the Fortune 500
have appeared on the list every time
since it has been published in 1955.

“We don't like their sound,
and guitar music is on the way out.”
Decca Recording Company rejecting The Beatles, 1962

IV
Crazy Normal

Marilyn vos Savant, who has the highest IQ ever recorded, 228, has a unique perspective regarding the masses and being crazy. 95.8% of the United States workers make less than $100,000 per year. They are the norm. Only 4.2% earn over $100,000. They are the abnormal or the crazy ones. Do you want to be a part of the masses, the norm, or the 4.2%, the abnormal few?

She says people who make under $100,000 are the masses and they live in a pocketbook dictionary world and the 4.2% live in an unabridged dictionary world. Pocketbook mentality means there is only one definition for every word. There is only one answer to each question, a fill-in-the-blanks mentality.

The unique few, the abnormal, live in an unabridged world where there are many answers and numerous definitions for each and every word. She says that life is a question that requires an essay answer. Most people unfortunately live in a world where whatever the masses say is what they believe. In other words, if someone were to call you crazy, in the normal world, that would be negative since it means deranged. In the abnormal world, the definitions may be positive, the exact opposite of what the norm believe and live by.

Look up the word crazy in an unabridged dictionary. You will see it also means: intensely enthusiastic; passionately excited; unusual; with great enthusiasm or energy; a nonconforming person.

Most people respond to external stimuli in a pre-programmed manner. We hear a word or a phrase and have a specific perspective based on our experiences. The interesting reality is most people never even think about this aspect of life. They use the simplest definitions, or whatever is the most commonly accepted usage. That is what they embrace. The sad part is that so much of their lives revolve around the same acceptance of mediocrity.

Think of how you would define: success, normal, opportunity, change, freedom, security, debt, money, job, belief, know, sure, cash, risk, mentor, partner, listen, love, see, money, genuine, teachable, challenge, hope, faith, genius, ready, done, leader, value, perspective, and credit. Maybe, a change of vocabulary is needed along with a change of thinking.

“Despite what you may believe, the most important relationship is with yourself. You've got one client. How are you doing?”

Dr. Phil McGraw: Over 1,000 success stories were studied by him.
Conclusions of what they all possessed: vision, strategy, take action, not risk averse, dealt with truth, passionate.

V
A vs B

Auto dealership A makes $1,000 per transaction and auto dealership B makes $10,000 per transaction. They buy the same brand of cars for the same price, sell the same cars for the same price, and sell the same number of cars with the same overhead per car. How is it possible?

Dealership A	Dealership B
$1,000 / Transaction	$10,000 / Transaction

A defines "T", a transaction as a car. B defines "T", a transaction as a relationship. Company B wants all the customer's business, not just the car sale. Parts, tires, body work, painting, warranty work, insurance, tinting, used cars – everything to do with new cars, plus their used car business as well. Company A focuses on the sale. Not on the person. They focus on volume of sales only.

Company B knows there are many more opportunities available with that one person. They see the direct lines of connectivity, their web of influence, as the person is sitting there. Everyone knows people you will never meet. You have one chance to meet them and that is if the customer wants you to.

This thinking pertains directly to real estate as well. If you only try to find people divorced, bankrupt, or in trouble, and try to steal their homes from them like the late-night-gurus teach, you will always be looking for another deal. You will have no repeat customers and absolutely no clients. If you employ a system that benefits the buyer, the seller and the ultimate end-user, referrals become part of your process and the power of compounding is able to exert its full force. The key is a duplicatable system.

When you date someone for the first time, if you treat them like a potential marriage partner, the date will be different and you never have to look back and say you wished you would have acted differently. A realtor sells one house to one person. The key is to find an investor who buys ten houses. The sale is the investor, not the house. The relationship is where the value is, not the sale of the house.

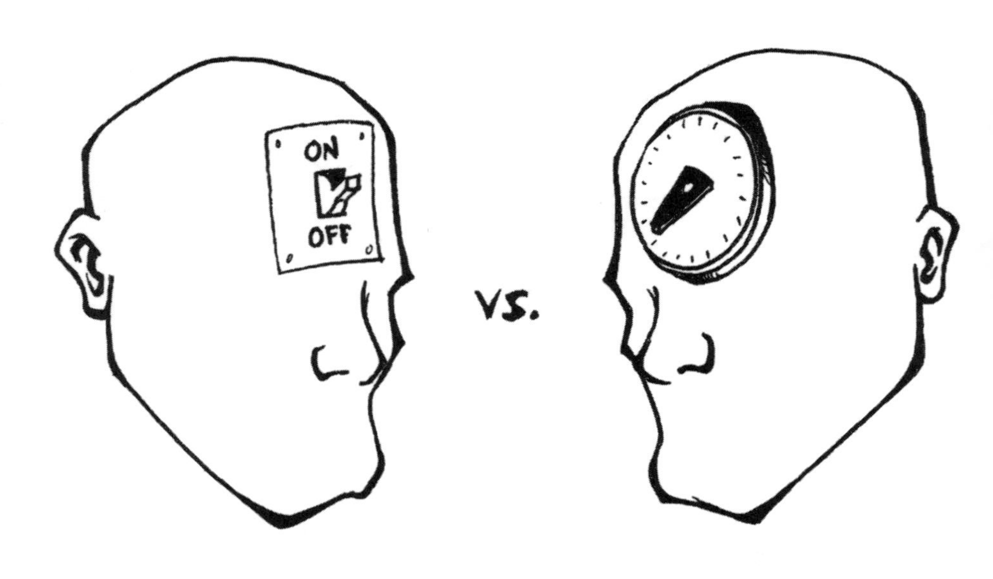
ON
OFF
VS.

VI
The Marriotts

Bill Marriott, Sr. started out owning a root beer stand, and turned it into a $30 million business with no debt. He abhored debt. He gave the business over to his son who immediately borrowed $30 million against his dad's assets. The father, when he learned about the debt, asked "How should I respond to that?" A truly elegant question. The son said, "Dad, what we owe today, we will be worth tomorrow, if we have an incoming producing asset that pays itself off." The primary difference is the philosophy of the business they saw themselves in.

Bill Jr. changed the company to $30 billion, the big "B". He changed what business they were in. The father bought land, built a building, and rented it out; a simple description of the hotel industry. The son did the same, except he sold the building to an investor for cash and took back a 75-year management contract and sold that for cash to Aetna and Travelers for their pension funds. Now, only one in 100 units with the Marriott name is actually owned by the Marriott Corporation. The other 99 are managed by them. They are now in the systems management business, not the hotel ownership business. More money is made in the processing than in the ownership, because of the ongoing, constant streams of income.

<u>Bill Marriott, Sr.</u>
$0 Debt
$30 million business
1. buy land
2. build a hotel
3. rent out

The hotel business

<u>Bill Marriott, Jr.</u>
$30 million in debt
$30 billion business
1. buy land
2. build a hotel
3. sell to investor for cash
4. take back 75-year mgt. contract, sell for cash

The systems management business

The philosophical difference is that the father was in the room rental business, and the son was in the business of processing room rental businesses. The son's perspective took the company from the "M" to the "B", the big Bill Gates "B", $30 billion, not $30 million.

Often people think what is needed to take them to the next level is a secret, a flick of a switch that will turn the lights on for them. However, in reality, its actually more like a slight turn of the dial. The Marriotts are experts at management because they have systematized the process.

“Great spirits have always encountered violent opposition from weak minds.”

Albert Einstein

VII
Female Drivers

When married couples come for consulting, there's usually a conservative and a liberal. The husband is typically the liberal, the "go for it", risk-taker type, and the wife is the mother, care giver, conservative, balancer, risk-averse person. Or, so she thinks. I like to show her that every day she takes more risks than her husband and instead of it involving money, it involves her life and her children's lives. The key is to change her perspective towards her definition of risk.

I like to paint a picture in her mind of her driving a car down a straightaway section of a highway. She assumes she is safe because she is in total control of her car which is seemingly going forward in a straight line. She travels 2 mph under the speed limit and does this every day. She is used to it. It probably seems to you at this stage, I have set up a difficult and challenging situation to use to prove she is not only reckless, but more of a liberal risk-taker than her husband will ever be.

You see the reality is she actually is never going in a straight line. She is constantly correcting her path. 45% of the time she is turning left, 45% of the time she is turning right, and only 10% of the time is the steering wheel actually going forward. She is constantly correcting her path.

It's really much safer to fly in airplanes than it is to travel in an automobile. There is only one death per million airline travelers, compared to one in 7,000 motor vehicle deaths. In a car you have control, but you are in a much more dangerous situation because you can only control yourself. 45% of the time mom is driving head-on toward a person doing exactly the same thing that she is doing. It seems safe while she is passing the person since she is only going 64 mph except the other car is just inches away from her.

Plus, she doesn't know if the other driver is drugged, suicidal, has a driver's license, or is falling asleep. Yet, she feels calm and safe enough to talk on the phone and hand food back to the kids. And, she feels her husband is the risk-taker since he goes for it in business all the time and risks their money.

Mom is used to what she does every single day. She doesn't focus on the risk. To her it is minimal. Her children are safe in seatbelts or car seats. She drives under the speed limit and unconditionally she feels safe. Maybe she is more liberal than she thinks.

ANY AFRICAN AMERICANS IN THE ROOM?
MOM

VIII
Sicilian American

I donate my time and books and speak in federal and state prisons and juvenile detention centers across the country. It's my charitable service work. The message I teach is the same as when I am speaking to a Fortune 500 Company or consulting one-on-one with a client – a perspective change is needed by everyone.

Typically about 200 inmates attend my presentations. The first thing I do when it's my time to start speaking, is go up to the biggest, meanest, blackest person in the room and loudly ask, "Are there any African Americans in the room today?" The room is quickly quieted awaiting the response. I now have their attention.

Some form of "Yeah, I am," will be directed back at me to which I in turn say, "You are so full of bologna. Is your mother from Africa? Is your father from Africa? Is your grandmother or grandfather from Africa? Have you even been or know where Africa is? My mother was born in Sicily and do you hear me introduce myself as, "Hello, my name is John Borzellino, I'm a Sicilian American?"

What gives you the right to call yourself an African American when no one in your family is from there? And what about you sir? (As I point to someone with Asian blood in them.) Are you an Asian American? Or you, are you a Mexican American?

All I am try to do is get them to think. We need to come together as a human race, not segregate ourselves. "I believe there are more African Americans prejudiced towards whites than the other way around and I have proof!" I tell them. "When did the black-white problem start, before or after 1960? Before of course. Well, there were only 3 billion people on the earth then and now there are 6 billion. Over half the people were born after 1960 and they all want to be mocha colored."

"I believe what we need is a good alien invasion. Do you remember in Will Smith's Independence Day movie when the aliens attacked? All of a sudden it was the humans against the aliens, not the Russians or the Chinese. Everyone came together as one. We as a human race need to do the same thing now and not wait for a catastrophe to force it to happen. We need to find more reasons why we are similar, not different." What makes the USA such a great and strong country is the diversity of its people. We are not a nation of pedigrees, but rather of mongers.

"I've always felt that if anyone is lucky enough to accumulate enough funds to live better than you have a right to, then you have a moral obligation to give something back."

Johnny Carson

All I want is for everyone to question their pre-programmed perspectives and think instead of react. Investors need to do the same thing. Zig Ziglar used to say, "If you keep doing what you've been doing, you will keep getting what you've been getting." And unless your income is doubling regularly, a change is what is necessary.

Think of a staircase. Where every step is double the previous step's income. If you made $50,000, the next step is $100,000 and so forth. The key is to bring someone down from way up the staircase to show you what to do one-on-one.

It's also important to note, any next step requires the same amount of effort and change. It may seem to get easier as you move up the staircase, but that is not true. Everyone, myself included, requires a 100% change to get to the next step. So often people think you can not remember what it was like to make under $100,000 since I made that when I was 19 years old. That perception is not true because evey step is a doubling step, and if your previous highest net was the step you are on, you haven't been to the next step ever.

If the most you have ever bench-pressed in your life was 200lbs, and the highest net yearly income you ever made was $100,000, proportionately to double either one requires 100% change. Remember the algebraic equation ratio A : B : : C : D? It means, A is to B as C is to D. Or, up is to down as fast is to slow.

A : B : : C : D
$100,000 : $200,000 : : 200lbs : 400lbs

For some reason, people think doubling one's income is easier than doubling a max bench press. Why? If you have never lifted over 200lbs, 201lbs seems impossible, and 400lbs is double your max. So, if I was hired as your consultant and the first thing I did was put 400lbs on the bench and said, "Now lift it, or I don't want to work with you!" What would you say? If you said I was crazy, remember what the unabridged definition of that word is: intensely enthusiastic, passionately excited, unusual, with great energy, with great speed, a nonconforming person. I would take it as a compliment, as a positive statement.

I would tell you, "I know you can do it." Would you then try? And afterward when you couldn't even budge it an inch, what would you say to me? "I can't." Instead, I want you to say, "I need your help." For that is the answer that is necessary to lift it. I never said you had to lift it yourself. With two spotters, one on each side helping, you would indeed be able to lift the weight. It is the same for doubling your income, you just need help as we all do to get to our next level, a level never before attained.

“I'm just glad it'll be Clark Gable who's falling on his face and not Gary Cooper.”

Said Gary Cooper on his
decision not to take the
leading role in “Gone with the Wind.”

IX
Compound Energy

Einsten said the strongest force in the universe is compounding. What does that mean and how can the principle be applied to real estate?

If you were presented with a choice of two consulting contracts, "I" would pay you $1,000 per day for 40 days or "II" would pay you a penny doubled everyday for 40 days.

Which would you pick?

I	II
$1,000	.01 – day 1
x 40 days	.02 – day 2
$40,000	.04 – day 3
	doubling every day
	for 40 days = ?

I like to use this example as an analogy for helping people realize their understanding of making money from real estate is way off from 'a better way'.

A : B : : C : D
A is to B as C is to D

A = your answer to what consulting contract II is worth
B = the correct answer
C = your knowledge of making money in real estate and your present highest net yearly income
D = the actual knowledge of making money from real estate and the cash available

What do you think "II" would equal after 40 days?

If your guess was $500, turn the page to see how far off you are compared to what is available to learn and make from real estate.

“People's thinking and perspectives will change dramatically in the years following 2000. People will feel the dawn of a new era and be ready for change.”

Bill Gates

1	.01	11	10.24	21	10,485.76	31	10,737,418.24
2	.02	12	20.48	22	20,971.52	32	21,474,836.48
3	.04	13	40.96	23	41,943.04	33	42,949,672.96
4	.08	14	81.92	24	83,886.08	34	85,899,345.92
5	.16	15	163.84	25	167,772.16	35	171,798,691.84
6	.32	16	327.98	26	335,544.32	36	343,597,383.68
7	.64	17	655.36	27	671,088.64	37	687,194,767.36
8	1.28	18	1,310.72	28	1,342,177.28	38	1,374,389,534.72
9	2.56	19	2,621.44	29	2,684,354.56	39	2,748,779,069.44
10	5.12	20	5,242.88	30	5,368,709.12	40	5,497,558,138.88
						TOTAL	$10,995,116,277.75

$11 Billion

Compound interest is interest on interest - A benefit on / of the benefit - A chain reaction of positive energy. Compounding is similar to a nuclear chain reaction. More energy is produced than is input and the rate of increase is exponential.

A sale of some sort is made and that buyer gives us a referral and so on. An event occurs that opens the door to massive opportunity. A club we join, a group we help out, a sport or hobby we take up – leads to new relationships, which increases the odds of interactions and connections. In order to create a constant stream of available new product, properties available to be purchased for 5-10% under appraisal, we need to get involved in activities outside of our normal life.

Activities like speaking, teaching, consulting, traveling, charity events, service work, group or association affiliations, etc. Living life in itself, creates opportunities to meet people who may be in a position, or have a desire to do business with us. Everyone wants to buy real estate when they get paid cash at closing!

"An individual's challenges, goals and desires can not be solved or reached by maintaining the same level of thinking one had when they were created."

Albert Einstein

CHECKS List Singly	DOLLARS	CENTS
1		
2		
3		
4		
5		
6		
7		
8		
9		
10		
11		
12		
13		
14		
15		
16		
17		
18		
19		
20		
21		
22		
23		
TOTAL		

ENTER TOTAL ON THE FRONT OF THIS SLIP

Checking Deposit

DATE____________ **NAME**____________________________

Use Other Side For
Additional Listing

CASH		
LIST CHECKS SINGLY		
TOTAL FROM OTHER SIDE		
TOTAL CHECKS & CASH		
LESS CASH RECEIVED		
TOTAL DEPOSIT		

____

Acknowledge Receipt of Cash Returned By Signing Above.

____

ACCOUNT NUMBER

1st Source Bank®

F0059TA Rev. 9/09

⑆551500020⑆ 20

X
Passion

Einstein's miracle year came in 1905. It's been written about Einstein, "Never before and never since has a single person enriched science by so much in such a short time as Einstein did." What would have happened if the year or day before 1905, he quit and gave up? How did he feel the minute, hour, day, or month just before 1905 started?

Passionate people aren't afraid of failing. Great scientific discoveries are not done deliberately, rather they occur serendipitously. This occurs with breakthroughs in finance as well. The activity, the churning of the system is what produces results.

Sir Issac Newton developed a form of mathematics called "calculus" in order to explain basic concepts in physics. When was the last time you invented something as a stepping stone to solve another challenge? When was the last time you learned something dramatic that you never even comprehended before? Like the penny doubled example. This knowledge of new information helps open ones mind to the possibility of what was before thought of only as seemingly impossible or improbable.

Passion is an energy forcefield that magnetizes people. It attracts them. Everyone can feel it. The person who possesses it is alive. They are full of energy. It is undeniable.

The top business people know the passion they feel for their product and service persuades the client to move ahead - since passion is the component that sells everything first. The top of any group, with the best attitude, have also learned the ability not to judge. Not to judge the situation ("Will they buy?" Or, "Won't they?"), and not to judge people, nor evoke their own set of rules, standards, morals and behaviors upon others.

When we learn to accept others by not judging, the spirit within us changes and our voice sings songs of hope. Our thoughts and behaviors project messages of optimism, an intangible characteristic within us that you can not touch, but others can feel. The same works with charm, charisma, class, gentlemanliness, and womanliness. When judgement does not exist, the good in someone else becomes obvious, negativity diminishes and optimism prevails.

“I think there is a world market for maybe five computers.”

Thomas Watson, chairman of IBM, 1943

When I teach in prisons, invariably a guard will come up to me after I was speaking to an inmate and say “Do you know what he (or she) is in here for?” At which I respond, “No thank you.” Who knows what that person did. If we think we do by judging them based on what the court said, what about the terrible things they wanted to do, but have not had the chance yet? Or, what about the things they did that no one knows about? For me, it is better to simply say they all made mistakes and lump them into that category instead of onto a scale telling me which inmate is better than another based on what they were convicted of.

Is a rapist more dangerous than a bank robber? What if the young man was in love and was planning on getting married? And the girl’s father was the judge, and she was just under 18 and this was 50 years ago? Would you feel differently then? How would you feel if you had judged the person according to what he was convicted of by a group of his peers? Who are your peers? I would never want a group of my “peers” to judge me on anything.

The same reason people don’t like to play Monopoly is why most people will never make any real money. It takes too long. But, not if you play “Turbo Monopoly”. The way you play is, as soon as the first person rolls the dice, the next person picks up the dice and rolls immediately. They do not wait for the first person to buy the property they landed on or to pay rent. Each person pays the bank for what they want to buy and everyone trusts each other. It’s a game. The idea is to have fun. No one is allowed to negotiate until all the properties are purchased.

Throw out the one dollar bills and round everything to the nearest $5.00 When you owe rent, put it in front of the person you owe it to. You do not wait for them to ask for it. The goal is to churn the system, get around the board and have all the properties purchased as fast as possible for that is when the real game starts.

After all the properties are purchased, whoever is holding the dice is allowed to speak or negotiate to buy or trade properties. No one else is allowed to speak or make a comment unless they are spoken to by the holder of the dice. When the negotiations are over, the dice is rolled and the next person now has their turn. If anyone comments negatively or positively about a negotiation, a fine of $500 is paid into the middle of the board and picked up by whoever lands on “free parking”.

The game can be finished in an hour. And, the game of real estate is similar. If you have a team and a system to work with, people who have a vested interest in you doing well, people who are of like mind, you can accomplish goals in a shorter time than previously only imagined.

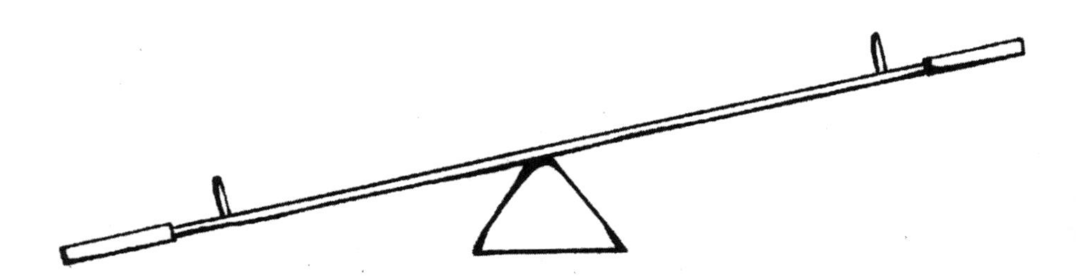

“The ability to shift perspective can be one
of the most powerful and effective tools
we have to cope with life's daily challenges.”

The Dalai Lama

XI
Granted Taken

We all take things for granted. At least we do until an event occurs like breaking a leg, or a bone, or loosing an eye, or finding out you need to wear glasses. Then, our perspective immediately changes.

Think of a see saw – our mind can change from one end to the other at the speed of light. Immediate changes can occur in our thinking. Some examples: you find out you are pregnant, you hit the lottery, you experience a life altering illness, or the loss of a close family member.

Some of the things we take for granted: the freedoms we enjoy in our country, our bodies (working properly or expecting them to regardless of what we do to them), families, or the ability to go in any direction in business, or to travel freely.

We never even think about hospitals unless we must go to one, or the value of police or fire fighters until we need one. The right and left hands working together, or our legs not stumbling when we walk or run. We just expect everything to work.

I was giving a speech one day and noticed a man in a wheel chair wheeling himself up to the front of the room. I immediately went over to him and asked what happened to put him in the chair. He later gave me a three page letter written in longhand thanking me for asking him, and acknowledging his existence.

He said most people ignore him totally. They divert their eyes and almost never speak to him. They rush around him, or stumble over him and never directly ask or speak to him. Sometimes the obvious is not always reality. People with challenges want to be included, not ignored or felt sorry for. From that day, every time I meet up with a person with a missing finger, an obvious scar, or in a wheelchair, I ask, "What happened?" So far, everyone has spoken kindly to me and seemed glad I noticed.

When these dramatic life altering events occur, we are presented with a choice, a defining life moment choice. New energy is available that we can use and direct if we so choose. But, why wait for something dramatic to occur to give us new energy? Let our new perspective give us the energy we need and direct it towards doubling our income.

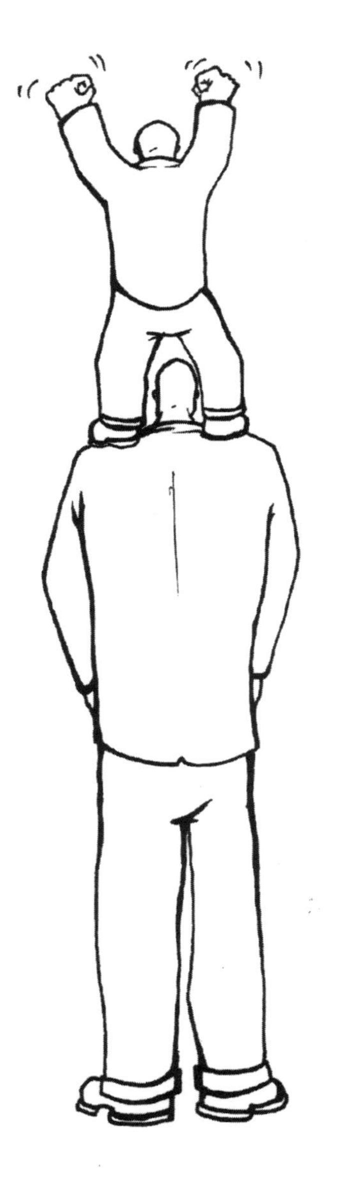

XII
Land of the Giants

I have been blessed with mentors all my life. My dad made over $250,000 per year. He bought real estate all his life so I was around it since I was a child. Another mentor of mine made $6 million a year and taught me how to hit 7-figures when I was 22 years old. My most recent mentor started a business with $72,000 and in eleven years sold it to American Express for $103 million in cash. His partner was Mr. Jerry Reinsdorf (Mr. R), the owner of the Chicago Bulls and White Sox. The company was Balcor.

Some excellent examples of high 7-digit thinking come directly from Mr. R as taught to me by my mentor. Mr. R owned a stock brokerage company and two of his top salespeople said they were the procurring cause of a certain $100,000 investor. The commission is 10% for bringing in an investor, however, both of his people said and felt they brought the investor in themselves.

What would you do?

Mr. R paid them both $10,000. If he would have only paid them $5,000 each, they would have felt slighted and unfairly compensated. Mr. R paid them out of his own pocket. Why? You never want to cause undue negativity in your top people. He knew they'd never done this before. They were not trying to take advantage of his kindness. They felt they were due and he paid them. He was making millions each year because of them and another $5,000 out of his pocket was worth keeping them happy.

Another example of higher level thinking is with his star player on the Bulls, Michael Jordan. When Michael quit the first time, he had over two years left on his contract. What could Mr. R have done? He could have sued Jordon for specific performance. What did he do? Not only did he not sue, but he gave Jordan the balance of his contract as a tip. When Michael came back to play again, where did he go? Right back to the Bulls. Mr. R made millions upon millions because of Michael. Most owners would have dealt with the "principle" issue and for sure not paid him and probably would have sued him. They would have indeed lost out when he returned.

Mentors are vital to us all. Tiger Woods went over two years without a coach and, without a victory. No one would have thought that possible. All the great scientists claim they have stood on the shoulders of giants when asked about their inventions.

"The highest forms of understanding
we can achieve are
laughter and human compassion."

Richard P. Feynman

Working with a mentor is like discovering the laws of six and seven figure thinking. An interesting analogy is someone trying to learn the laws of chess merely by observing chess games. You notice that bishops stay on the same color squares; you write this down as a law of chess. Later, you come up with a better law – bishops move diagonally. And, since diagonal squares are always colored the same, this explains why bishops always stay on the same color. This law is an improvement, it is simpler, and yet it explains more. However, having a coach explain it to you, compresses the time it takes to learn the game. And, most importantly, teaches you things never written in a book.

Contrary to popular wisdom, business start-ups soar when the economy sours. That is because laid-off workers like Disney, convinced they've got great ideas, pursue self-employment. Disney, despite a rocky start, believed animation couldn't lose. Two years before starting work in his uncle's garage, Disney's Laugh-O-Gram Films venture went bust. Workers abandoned him, and he barely had enough to eat.

“I see hope in every cloud.”
Elton John

XIII
Friction Solution

Friction, adversity, and pain cause some people to break, and others to break records. How does it feel for a beginner having a difficult time skiing, when they are passed by a one-legged skier or by a blind skier?

Adversity is vital. Many of us want to end all adversity; end the difficult and only experience the simple, the easy, the no-effort way. This is just against nature, and why the late night gurus sell millions of get-rich-quick programs. People want to skip the planting process and just harvest their crops.

Adversity is friction. Friction is necessary. Many times it is an indicator that things are about to go positive, stratospheric, to the next level. It's similar to a plateau in losing weight. You may just be building the energy to jump to your next level.

Adversity, challenges and suffering builds integrity and actually serves as a source of energy for us to maintain our focus and achieve our destiny. When we face adversity, we are strained in our ability to maintain. When we do succeed, we are strengthened because we have learned how to deal with that particular aspect of life. The issue here is that we do not change our focus, we do not take a detour, we do not ignore, but rather we go through adversity. In the process of doing so, we learn about ourselves. We learn how to approach and maintain our path to our destiny.

Erik Weihenmayer was the first blind person to climb the tallest peaks on all seven continents. He said he hopes to show people that what may seem unattainable is really within reach. He was a former middle school teacher and wrestling coach, and started climbing after losing his sight to a rare eye disease at age 13.

No matter how many businesses or properties you have tried to make work in the past and seemingly failed, you now know what not to do. Experience is the best educator of all.

“This 'telephone' has too
many shortcomings to be seriously
considered as a means of communication.
The device is inherently of no value to us.”

Western Union internal memo, 1876

XIV
Hold the Fleas

A research experiment was conducted where sharks were placed in a big aquarium fish tank and fed. A plexiglass wall was lowered separating the new food from the sharks. The sharks bashed their heads against the wall so many times that they eventually quit trying to eat. Eventually, the wall was raised and the sharks refused to try to get to the food anymore and starved themselves to death. Unknowingly, they were inches away from their sustinence. This is similar in perspective to people who are so close to success, but they quit too soon.

How is it possible for circus performers to control one of the strongest animals on earth, the elephant, with just a small rope? When they are babies, they put a big, thick, strong chain around its neck and cement it into the ground. The animal tugs and pulls, and it eventually stops trying to get anywhere because of the number of failures, and the pain in its neck. The elephant becomes conditioned.

Another experiment was conducted where jumping fleas were put into a small empty fish aquarium. A lid was put on top. The fleas jumped and jumped, banging their heads so many times, they quit jumping. They became controlled by their experiences, by others, by the odds. The experiment changed the belief of the jumping fleas to the point where they didn't believe they could jump anymore. So they just stopped. The lid was taken off and the fleas never jumped out.

These are examples that lead to a very primitive reptilian brain-type learning in which if one does not succeed, one stops trying. This is reptilian because humans don't have to act this way. In other words, humans don't know any better that when they keep failing, they can just keep trying harder and success may be just around the corner. Humans are able to focus beyond the horizon, such that any adversity including a plexiglas shield keeping one away from food is merely a nuisance, and not a learning mechanism.

“To every man is given the key to the gates of heaven, the same key opens the gates to hell.”

Proverb of the Buddhist religion

XV
Discipline Me Not

Sam Walton began with a single dime store in 1945 and did not open his second store for seven years. Twenty-five years later, Wal-Mart had only 38 stores. Today, Wal-Mart has about 4,000 stores, building up to that number through a process that has been slow and steady. Over seven decades the $72,000 Sam started with has turned into a $1 trillion corporation.

You achieve greatness in much the same way that you turn a giant gear or flywheel. It takes a huge amount of effort to get the thing moving from one turn to two, but if you keep pushing in a consistent direction, you'll eventually hit a hundred, then a thousand, then a million RPMs. When you combine a consistent direction with substantial speed, you achieve something greater than either of those elements alone - momentum.

The next time you are waiting for the light to turn green and it turns and the person in front of you doesn't move, just sit there and wait. Don't honk your horn or get steamed. See how unique it feels. Remember the definition of a New York second? The time it takes for the person behind you to honk after the light turns green.

Superstars all felt like their breakthrough was always right around the corner. And they all said, "There was a time I almost gave it all up". However, they persevered. That is why they have a story to tell. When you live with the feeling that you are a phone call away from a dramatic change, the opportunity, the big deal, the major connection, your energy and countenance show it. It's magnetic.

The mindset of great athletes is amazing. A confident hitter swaggers up to the plate with the intent to kill the ball. It's the same for pitchers and for race car drivers. The key is the concept of perseverance helping to make a breakthrough when all the odds were against it. In 1954, Roger Bannister broke the 4-minute mile and within 1 year, 37 runners broke his record. Why? Because they now had a reference that it could be done. Certainty generates the momentum for powerful beliefs. Anything can be accomplished when it is known that it has already been done before.

If he can do it, so can I. Accomplishing the impossible – it is only impossible until everyone believes it can't be done, then a believer shows up who changes everything. Lance Armstrong is the modern-day example of this. He just believed he was going to win and he did seven times in a row.

"I have traveled the length and breadth of this country and talked with the best people, and I can assure you that data processing is a fad that won't last out the year."

The editor in charge of business books for
Prentice Hall, 1957

XVI
Basic Rules

When driving a car, never back out further than you need to.

Always let the people on the elevator off first (before getting on yourself).

Rule #1 – if it can possibly do some good and it can't do any harm, do it.

Rule #7 - Don't take yourself too seriously.

Expect to make it huge, not just big.

While driving your car, if you are going to cut in front of someone anyway, at least wave and say 'Thank you!'.

Always wave to police and fireman.

Take up a musical instrument.

Exercise, or at least take walks.

Write in a journal / write your autobiography.

Never – doubt, judge, complain, wait to see what happens, or blame.

Always - appreciate, believe, expect the best, push yourself, start from now, count your blessings, take responsibility, forgive, and compound and compress.

Whenever you hit a bad shot in golf, put down another ball and hit it again. Never keep score unless you are in a tournament or working on your average. Set your tee time for 8am and play the back nine. No one will be ahead of you and no one will be behind you. If you hit 3 or 4 balls each time to get a good shot, you will actually play 2 full rounds in 9 holes. Plus, you will be getting much better.

HIT A HOME RUN!!!

XVII
Little Joey

The first time Joey is up to bat in a game of baseball, his father is standing behind the batting cage yelling,

"Hit a home run!"

Let's analyze the 13 steps Joey would miss if he listened to his dad.

1. develop a love for, or a desire to play the game
2. find a good coach
3. practice
4. learn to accept failure as a huge part of the game
5. treat every at bat as though you will get a hit
6. get to the plate and watch the ball
7. swing hard in case you hit it
8. touch the ball
9. hit the ball foul
10. hit the ball fair and get caught or thrown out
11. get a fair hit and get on first base
12. get on second
13. get on third
14. hit a home run

Joey can only control two things: his bat and whether he swings. He can't control the fielders positions, the weather, the pitcher's skill, or choice of pitches. All he can control is where and when he swings the bat. Even after he makes contact with the ball, he has no control over the defense. He needs to spend time on what he can control and focus. He can also control his: temperment, motivation, willingness to succeed and block out the rest.

Investors need to realize there are many steps prior to getting a home-run deal. Too often they want to skip the steps that are necessary. It's important to know that there are perspective changes that must occur before the income has the energy or the ability to double.

“When a true genius appears in this world, you may know him by this sign: that the dunces are all in confederacy against him.”

Jonathan Swift

XVIII
Genius

Marilyn vos Savant says creativity is necessary for genius, but not sufficient: the creation must shatter worlds and bring forth new ones. Geniuses do not merely solve existing problems, like discovering an AIDS cure. They identify new ones.

“Before I started composing recently, my brain was feeling out strings of pieces from my childhood, little scraps of melody that I would hear and remember. I feed it and feed it and it all subconsciously comes together,” said a composer.

It is called the permutation of “mental elements” – images, phrases, snippets of memory, abstract concepts, sounds and rhymes. Intelligence fills the brain with more of these elements; like the child with pailfulls of Legos, the highly intelligent person has a greater chance of forming the novel combinations of ideas, images or symbols that constitute a masterpiece than does someone with a mere starter set.

Geniuses are geniuses because they form more novel combinations than the merely talented. They entertain permutations of images and memories that more mundane thinkers toss out as too strange. Creative geniuses are willing to take intellectual risks by merging disparate ideas. They discard accepted ideas of what’s possible making it easier to take new ideas more seriously.

Scientific genius is often marked by an interest in unrelated fields. They are always curious, and interested. They have an almost childlike enthusiasm for work, especially for wonders created by extraordinary minds. If one style of thought stands out as the most potent explanation of genius, it is the ability to make juxtapositions that elude mere mortals. They possess the ability to connect the unconnected, to see relationships to which others are blind.

In the building of a piece of music, there is not music at all – musicians type out descriptions and do drawings, and sometimes just shapes. The creative geniuses of art and science work obsessively. They do not lounge under apple trees waiting for fruit to fall, or lightning to strike. “When inspiration does not come to me”, Freud wrote, “I go halfway to meet it.” In a study of scientists, it was found that the most respected produced not only more great works, but also more “bad” ones. They produced, period.

“Crazy people who are productive are geniuses.
Crazy people who are rich are eccentric.
Crazy people who are neither productive
nor rich are just plain crazy.”

Michael Gelb

Creative geniuses tend to return to the conceptual world of childhood, to wed the most advanced understandings of a field with the kinds of problems, questions, issues and sensibilities that most characterize a wonder-filled child. It is a particular combination of youth and maturity that allows the most revolutionary work to take place in the sciences. Too much time and experience thinking in a certain way can prove uncongenial to any innovation.

Put another way, as the once chance permutations of ideas and images harden in the mind, the intellect becomes so set, so organized, that there are fewer stray elements and fewer chances for spontaneous, novel combinations. It's been called the "self-defeating aspect of creativity." "When I was younger I would wake up every morning with the feeling that I was going to have a better idea that day than I had ever had before," an inventor said.

"The concept is interesting and well formed,
but in order to earn better than a "C",
the idea must be feasible."

A Yale University Management Professor
in response to Fred Smith's paper
proposing reliable overnight delivery
service. Smith went on to found FedEx.

“Genius is the ability to reduce the complicated to the simple.”

C. W. Ceram

IX
Mensa Lied

If you found out you were a literal genius, would your perspective towards yourself and those around you change? If so, how? My premise is that all of a sudden, you would listen to your intuitions. Your ideas would take shape more. Your thinking would seem more valuable. People would listen more to you even if they didn't know your IQ score because the genius person would dramatically be altered positively. Thoughts would be written down. Chances would be taken. Odds would be increased.

All of us are geniuses.

If the standard thinking is people use only 10% of their brains, and they accomplish an average IQ (100) with only 10% usage, what is happening to the other 90%? Isn't it still there, meaning they have way more than genius in them already? If your parents had opened a savings account for you at birth and put in one million dollars and you didn't know about it, aren't you a millionaire even though you don't know it?

What percentage of a person's brain needs to be utilized to get to the score of genius? Probably only another 4% that is all. How do you tap into that extra 4%? A dramatic change of negative or positive can help. In times of war, divorce, or a close relative's death, a person must tap into other resources to survive and deal with their new reality. There is nowhere to run and hide. They must dig down deep within themselves and muster up the energy and wherewithall to not only handle, but master the situation they find themselves in.

On the matter of genius, American Mensa, The High IQ Society, has said that an IQ of 140 means you are a genius. However, there is no such definition in psychological testing. There are also no reputable test publishers that would use an IQ score to classify someone in that category. The 140 IQ is probably a misunderstanding that dates back to when Terman conducted research with several students with IQ's above 140. From subsequent reporting about the study, the magic figure of IQ 140 came into play.

There are some individuals that probably are geniuses in the sense that they have superior intelligence, such as Einstein and Edison. Interestingly, testing reveals that highly creative people often do poorly on standardized tests because they use their test time thinking of broader applications to simple questions.

-1
2+2=5

2 + 2 = 5 – 1

If you aswered the 2 + 2 question with the above answer, you would be marked wrong. Or, if you answered with the square root of 16, you also would be marked wrong. Even though there may be a second right answer, mass standardized testing has made us a society of fill-in-the-blanks, true-or-false, yes-or-no people. When in actuality, most of life's questions need essay answers.

It's imprtant to note, both Edison and Einstein were failures in public schools and did poorly on exams. Nobel prize winners are obviously brilliant thinkers and creators at a superior level, but whether their abilities could be measured with a standardized test is a mystery.

EQ vs IQ

EQ, the emotional quotient, is a form of intelligence relating to the emotional side of life, such as the ability to recognize, and manage one's own and other's emotions, to motivate oneself, and restrain impulses and to handle interpersonal relationships effectively. Neurological pathways in the brain generate an emotion and generate the reaction to an emotion. Stress and constant threats rewire emotional circuits. How we evaluate information leads to how we will respond, our behavior and our body language. Our evaluations of what we experience create our personal reality.

What's intelligence? IQ is simply defined as the type of test utilized in measuring intelligence. There are social intelligence scales, which deal with social interaction ability. There is street smarts intelligence. There is athletic intelligence. There is also intelligence in terms of survival, which is very useful in terms of the military and other types of such operations.

I believe everyone is a genius. Just because you may not know how to open up another 4% does not mean you don't already possess the ability.

“Children are adults in little bodies
and adults are children in big bodies.”

Mr. Mentor

XX
Ponder This

Two women apply for jobs. They look exactly alike. On their applications they list the same last name, address and phone number. They were born to the same parents, on the same day, same month, same year. Everything is identical. The receptionist says, “You must be twins?” And they say, “No.” - How is that possible? [1]

What about non-random chance?

Why not realize nothing is too good to be true?

Is it really always better to be safe than sorry?

Do you doubt your doubts?

What question can you never answer “Yes” to?[2]

Where is there no south, east or west? – Every way you look is north.[3]

Joe and Mary both say they are the center of the universe. Who is right, who is wrong and why?[4]

Answers

1 – They are triplets
2 – Are you asleep? Are you dead?
3 – The South pole
4 – They both are correct since the commonly accepted thinking is that the universe is expanding equally in all directions.

“Stocks have reached what looks like a permanently high plateau.”

Irving Fisher, Professor of Economics,
Yale University, 1929

XXI
Think

If you are 30 today and you are going to live to only be 35, how old are you really compared to your life expectancy? If life expectancy is 74, then are you really 71? If you expect to live to be 105, and you are really 42, should you feel 23?

Why do all the books, Stephen Hawking's included, say "light speed is the fastest anything can travel"? Instead, after all the revelations and contradictions (flat earth), shouldn't it be said, 'That is known to man at the time of this printing'?

Warren Buffet's mentor made the majority of his decisions with how he felt. Going with how you feel may have much more merit than before thought.

Einstein worked in the morning and then sailed in the afternoon, rain or shine, Einstein would sail. At that point he became centered within himself. The forces of the wind, the water, and all other forces known and unknown, impinged upon Albert as he was in his boat dealing with all these forces. It is within this context, it's been said, that Einstein had the greatest revelations. It wasn't to control; it was rather just to experience, to be with the simplicity, and the elegance of nature.

Why do birds fly in formation? Because the birds that follow the leader have an easier flight. The leader breaks the wind resistance, and the following birds can fly far more efficiently. Without the triangle formation, Canadian geese would never have enough energy to make it to the end of their long migration.

Anyone who wants to trade a financial instrument has to pay the owner a royalty. If you buy or sell options on the Standard & Poor's 500 stock index, for example, about 10 cents per trade (the precise amount is a big secret) goes to McGraw-Hill, owner of the Standard & Poor's trademark. Want to trade options on the Dow Jones Industrial Average? That will require a small per-trade payment to the *Wall Street Journal*.

Multiply that payment by the more than 1.5 billion DJIA options and future contracts sold at just the Chicago Board of Trade in just a single month and you can see that owning a financial instrument can produce significant revenue.

Wouldn't it be nice to have a voice mail message that tells the truth - "I will call you back if I feel like it"?

Walt Disney lost his acting job and started his cartoon company in a Hollywood garage.
Timing 1923-4 recession

Sixteen of the 30 corporations in the Dow Jones industrial average trace their birth to recessions.

Common sense should be called "uncommon sense."

John Daly won the Buick Invitational in 2004, winning $864,000, which was approximately 1/3 of his winnings over the last 10 years. He won the tournament six months after learning his fourth wife had been indicted on federal drug and gambling charges, just five days after giving birth to his first son. His ranking had plunged to #299 in the world. 'His life was a mess' – wrote the sports writers. "I never doubted I could win," said Daly who had gone 189 Tournament events without a single victory.

I had a dream where bad guys were chasing me and I was barely eluding them until they eventually caught up with me and there was no way out, and like a switch went off, I broke character and said, "Okay, let's do that scene again this way." As if the chase was fake and was part of a movie pilot that we were filming and I was the actor / director who was in charge instead of the frightened victim. There was just no way for me to get out of the situation except to call "Cut!" Sometimes you just have to yell, "Cut!"

Remember: amateurs built the ark ... professionals built the Titanic.

The opposite of love is indifference, not hate.

When I talk about using your mind, ultimately it's to use your mind to carbonate your emotions and imagination. You know, how soda is carbonated. It's not just flat in the glass; it's filled with bubbles rising, bumping into each other, bursting, alive. That's the point of everything I'm teaching you – to make you not act, but live.

In the history of science, great breakthroughs often occur when someone realizes that two situations thought to be different are actually the same.

A question of thought was asked "How many pennies would it take to fill up this room?" and a potential employee at the interview asked in return "With or without us in the room?" I love when I hear brilliant spontaneous thinking so eloquently delivered.

As time passes, the perspective of "If I only had my old problem that I thought was so bad. What I wouldn't do to trade it for what I am dealing with right now." Since almost everyone can relate to this statement, shouldn't we all realize "Nothing is as bad as it seems than at the time that it happens." And, realize problems are really just challenges.

37

I met a man who had the blues, For on his feet he had no shoes.
Until upon the street, He met a man who had no feet.

When asked what class he would teach if he could at a theatre school, Orson Wells said he would teach life, nothing about movies. Life experiences, traveling ... are more valuable than any book knowledge and degrees.

An English professor once wrote on the blackboard: Punctuate this sentence -

'Woman without her man is nothing'.

The men wrote: "Woman, without her man, is nothing."
The women wrote: Woman! Without her, man is nothing."

When you are driving on the 65mph highway, how fast are you comfortable driving? 70, 75, 80, 85? What do you feel about the driver who passes you going 95mph? Or 100mph? Is he, really speeding? How do you think the driver of the person you passed going 65mph feels about you?

The odds of winning the lottery are the same likelihood as walking out your front door and getting hit by a meteorite. The only question you should ask yourself is –

"When you leave home, do you look up?"

There is a story of a young man applying for a job at a telegraph office. When he arrived for his interview, he noticed a few other applicants sitting, waiting near the boss' door. He went to the main window, identified himself over the chatter and tick tick tick of the telegraph and was told to sit down and wait for further instruction. After a few minutes he got up and entered the boss' office unannounced. The boss came out and told the other applicants that the job was filled. One of the other applicants questioned why they weren't given the chance to formally interview when they had arrived before the person who was granted the job. The boss simply stated "Did you listen to the telegraph?" at that point everyone else realized that what they heard as background noise was a telegraph message to go into the boss' office as soon as you hear this.

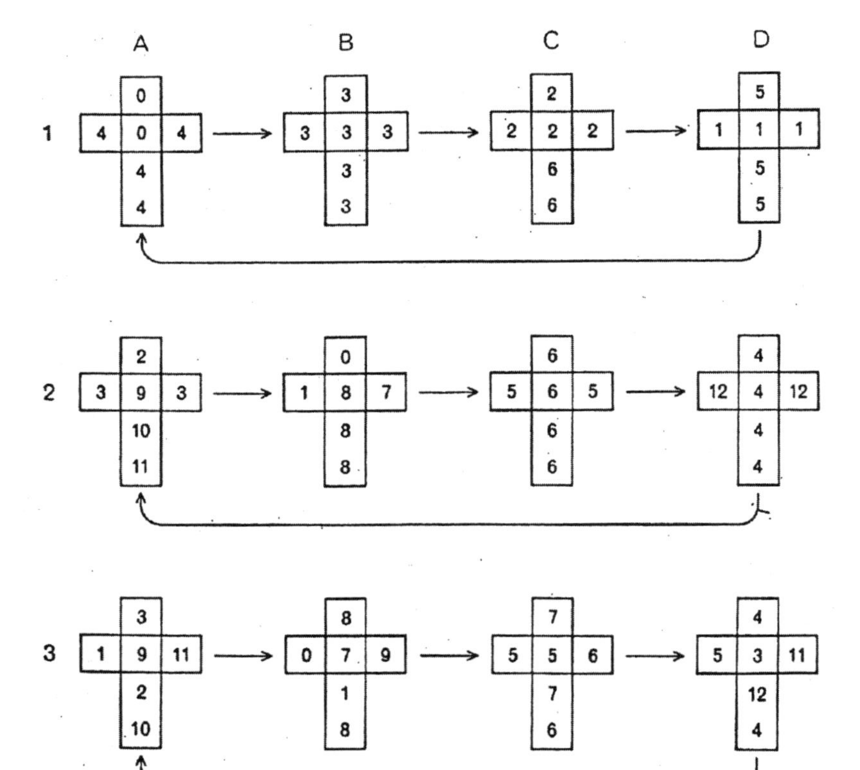

A
B
C
D
1
2
3
0 4 0 4 4 4
3 3 3 3 3 3
2 2 2 2 6 6
5 1 1 1 5 5
2 3 9 3 10 11
0 1 8 7 8 8
6 5 6 5 6 6
4 12 4 12 4 4
3 1 9 11 2 10
8 0 7 9 1 8
7 5 5 6 7 6
4 5 3 11 12 4

XXII
Throw the Dice

The paradox of the nontransitive dice and the elusive principle of indifference. Transitivity is the binary relation of such that if it holds between A and B and between B and C, it must also hold between A and C. A common example is the relation “heavier than”. If A is heavier than B and B is heavier than C, then A is heavier than C.

Bradley Efron, a statistician at Stanford University, designed the three sets of four dice shown “unfolded” in the illustration to dramatize some recent discoveries about a general class of probability paradoxes that violate transitivity. With any of his sets of dice, you can operate a betting game so contrary to intuition that experienced gamblers will find it almost impossible to comprehend even after they have completely analyzed it.

Allow someone to pick any die from this set. You then select a die from the remaining three. Both dice are tossed and the person who gets the highest number wins. Surely, it seems if your opponent is allowed the first choice of a die before each contest, the game must either be fair or favor your opponent. If at least two dice have equal and maximum probabilities of winning, the game is fair because if he picks one such die, you can pick the other; if one die is better than the other three, your opponent can always choose that die and win more than half of the contests. This reasoning is completely wrong. The incredible truth is that regardless of which die he picks you can always pick a die that has a 2/3 probability of winning, or two-to-one odds in your favor!

The paradox (insofar as it violates common sense) arises from the mistaken assumption that the relation “more likely to win” must be transitive between pairs of dice. This is not the case with any of the three sets of dice. In each set an arrow that points to the losing die indicates the relation “more likely to win”. Die A beats B, B beats C, C beats D – and D beats A! In the first set the probability of winning with the indicated die of each pair is 2/3.

There is no best, only better. The perspective you have on real estate and the methodology you are presently using is not necessarily bad, but there may be better.

“The harder I work,
the luckier I get.”

Arnold Palmer

XXIII
Lucky Dog

Luck isn't due to kismet, karma, or coincidence. Instead, lucky folks – without even knowing it – think and behave in ways that create good fortune in their lives. When things go awry, the lucky "turn bad luck into good" by seeing how they can squeeze some benefit from the misfortune. Lucky people are particularly open to possibility. Most people are just not open to what's around them. We have far more control over events than we thought previously. You might say 'a big percentage of my life is due to chance events'. No, it's not. Maybe 10% is. That other big chunk of brain that you think you're having no influence over at all is actually defined by the way you think.

Lucky people are open to new experiences. Unlucky people are stuck in routines. When they see something new, they want no part of it. Lucky people always want something new. They're prepared to take risks and they are relaxed enough to see the opportunities in the first place. Some other ways lucky people's minds operate differently: they practice "counterfactual thinking." The degree to which you think that something is fortunate or not is the degree to which you generate alternatives that are better or worse. Unlucky people say "I can't believe I've been in another car accident." Lucky people go, "Yes, I had a car accident, but I wasn't killed. And I met the guy in the other car, and there might be a relationship there."

What's interesting is that both ways of thinking are unconscious and automatic. It would never occur to unlucky people to see it a different way. Can we acknowledge that sometimes bad stuff, car accidents, and natural disasters just happen? Sometimes it's purely bad, and there's nothing good about it. No lucky person has ever said that. So if you buy into that way of thinking, then there is no bad luck. Lucky people have dreadful stories, but feel and look at them entirely differently.

There is a study showing people who are lucky are observant and see opportunity. People who are unlucky don't take risks because they don't see opportunity. People who are unlucky use repetitive behavioral patterns to maintain safety, and therefore limit themselves, and cannot even see, or observe, or be aware of opportunity.

By embracing new experiences and varying your routine, you throw yourself in serendipity's way, increasing your odds of getting a lucky break. Unlucky people try too hard to analyze everything. Lucky folks make intuitive decisions. They shoot from the hip. Even Benjamin Graham, Warren Buffet's mentor and the greatest investment thinker of all time, owed much of his fame and fortune to a hunch.

“Iron rusts from disuse;
water loses its purity from stagnation …
even so does inaction sap the vigor of the mind.”

Leonardo Da Vinci

XXIV
Obsession

In the movie, The Bridge on the River Kwai, the lead character, Colonel Nicholson (played by Alec Guinness) is a prisoner of war in Burma who must build a bridge for his Japanese captors. He builds a spectacular bridge and toward the end of the film, defends it from his officers who want to destroy it so the Japanese trains could not use it. A moment of realization comes to him when just before blowing it up; he says the famous line "What have I done?" He was so focused on his immediate goal of building the bridge, that he forgot his larger mission of winning the war. The bridge building became his goal obsession.

Most people find themselves in this situation. Focusing so much on the short-term immediate goal that they forget the larger long-term goal. Then, ten or twenty years later, they find nothing in their life has changed.

An excellent example of goal obsession was the "Good Samaritan" research project done at Princeton in 1973. A group of theology students was told they needed to go across campus to give a sermon on the Good Samaritan parable from the Bible. Part of the research was telling some of the students they were late and needed to hurry to the other side of campus. An actor was hired to pretend to be a victim who was hurt and in need, similar to the Biblical story.

90% of the "late" students, who were part of the Theology Seminary Program, ignored the actor and rushed to give their speech. The study reported that many of these theology students had to step over the victim as they rushed to their goal. Why? Goal obsession clouded their judgment. They focused on the smaller mission of building the bridge and not winning the war.

We all must step back, breath, reevaluate, reflect, relax and think. What do we really want? What are we doing? Why? Are we achieving the immediate task and forgetting our ultimate goals?

We don't want to be ten years down the road saying to ourselves,

"What have I done?"

“Not everything that counts can be counted,
and not everything that can be counted, counts.”

Sign hanging in Albert Einstein's office at Princeton

XXV
Fourth of July

The decision to hold the Continental Congress in Philadelphia on September 5, 1774 is much more important than July 4, 1776. If there had been no decision to hold the Congress, there would be no signing of the Declaration of Independence.

After Thomas Jefferson wrote "Summary View of the Rights of British America" he was told he was going to be prosecuted for high treason against His Majesty's government. Patrick Henry spoke his famous line at that time,

"If this be treason, then make the most of it."

This type of man, with no power, no authority, no army, no money, only interested in the colonies destiny that made the difference for all of us today and forever. Richard Henry made a motion stating,

"Gentlemen, I make the motion that these United Colonies, ought to be free and independent states ..."

The motion was discussed to death. After what seemed like forever, he took the floor again and said "Mr. President, we have discussed this issue for days. It is the only course to follow ... let this happy day give birth to an American Republic. Let her arise, not to devastate and to conquer, but to reestablish the reign of peace, and of law."

Before his motion was voted on, he had to leave for a family emergency. He placed his cause in the hands of Thomas Jefferson as chairman of the committee to draw up the Declaration of Independence. After a long struggle with the specifics of the document, one was drafted that ensured every man signing it was really signing his own death warrant if the colonies were to lose in a fight with Great Britain that was ultimately about to occur.

On July 4, 1776 Thomas Jefferson stood before the assembly and read the most important document ever recorded on paper.

"When in the course of human events it becomes necessary for one people to dissolve the political bands ..."

Famous people fired from jobs:

Donald Trump, Lou Holtz (head of Univ. NC), Bernie Marcus (founder of Home Depot), Jesse Ventura, Larry King, Lee Iacocca, Michael Bloomberg (mayor of NYC), Billie Jean King, Muhammad Ali, Robert Redford

A nation of decision makers was born when the 56 men signed it. Their spirit and courage gave Washington's armies the drive inside their hearts transforming into a spiritual power to accept only success.

That same power can be used by anyone who wants to become self-determining. It is an eternal law of nature. One must reach decisions promptly and definitely. Leaders of every type, decide quickly and firmly. This is a major reason they are leaders.

98 out of 100 people employed work in dead-end positions because they lack definiteness of decision. It requires courage. The signers of the Declaration of Independence staked their lives on the decision to sign. Anyone who reaches this definite decision level in life as an entrepreneur, probably never needs to stake his life, he stakes his economic freedom. The person, who desires wealth with spirit, is sure to achieve it.

"There is an uncommon joy
that comes with limitless potential."
Unknown

“What is mathematics?
Mathematics is looking for the patterns.”
Richard P. Feynman

XXVI
Professor Feynman

Professor Richard P. Feynman is one of my favorite physicists. He gave an example of an ape. The ape had only two measurable skills – pushing things around with a stick and reaching for things through the bars of its cage. He put a banana out of reach on the floor outside the bars to its cage and after awhile the ape rolled over in frustration. After a period of time, it tried again by discovering that by putting two disparate ideas together, it turned the old tool, the stick, into an altogether different kind of tool. Just like Galileo did with the telescope which had been invented as a toy, to look at the sky.

Many discoveries are like that, new ways of looking at old things, or concepts. But, the raw materials for the discovery was always there, which is why the discoveries may seem startling at the time, but are simple and obvious to later generations.

Feynman on discoveries, "I fool myself into thinking I have an extra chance. I am not the exact same as anyone else. I always think I have an inside track. I always try another way. I convince myself others are not doing it right and I am going to do it a different way. I talk myself into things and I get myself excited and enthusiastic."

When there is a hard problem, one has to work a long time and has to be persistent. In order to be persistent, you have got to be convinced that it's worthwhile working so hard, that you are going to get somewhere. And that takes a certain kind of fooling yourself. Imagination and persistence are important to making anything happen.

To solve a great physics research problem, involves approximation upon approximation, assumption upon assumption and those great leaps of imagination people call thinking outside the box. It involves the ability to move forward, follow your intuition and accept that you don't fully understand what you are doing. And, most entails believing in yourself. Feynman used powerful imagination to solve his physics problems combined with his Babylonian style.

He explained – the creative mind has a vast attic. The homework problem you did in college, the seemingly pointless paper you did in high school, an off-hand remark by a colleague, all are stored in hope chests somewhere up in a creative person's brain, often to be picked through and applied by the subconscious at the most unexpected moments.

XXVII
Reverse Logic

To get better at playing pool, is it better to play against people you can always beat, people not as good as you; Or, is it better to play against people better than you, people that will always beat you?

Using reverse logic it is not only possible, but probable by playing people not as good as you. Most authorities will say the opposite. The key ingredient, or premise – always shoot the hardest shot on the table. If you are playing someone better than you, you will shoot the easiest shots and never get better because you would never attempt the most difficult shots you might miss. Since you want to win, you will shoot the easiest ones and you could actually end up regressing in your skill level. Therefore, it is actually better to play people that are not as good as you as long as you shoot the hardest shots to keep the game interesting. I discovered this playing against my wife. I now sometimes watch my double banks go in.

There is beauty in simplistic elegance. I used to play the teaching tennis pros at clubs in the towns I was touring. I paid to play and if I won I did not have to pay. Regardless, I wanted them to give me one piece of advice or suggestion to help improve my game. One pro said, "I am going to give you a piece of advice learned from my mentor and now passed on to you since I really believe you want to learn and will listen to what I have to say." That was key to the advice he gave me. "It will improve your game by at least 10% maybe up to 25% for the rest of your life." He had my interest and my ears and my focus. "Never try to win return of service."

The reason is because the serve is sometimes coming at 95mph and too often when trying to hit the ball back with force and accuracy, it simply results in an unforced error. By conceding the fact that it is fruitless to attempt to win a point on return of service due to your non-skillful return, you actually not only dramatically reduce your unforced errors, but the change of pace from just getting it over the net often causes the server to be the one to make the unforced error.

There was an engineer who was hired by the owner of a large financial institution to fix his mainframe computer. He walked into the company, went up to the mainframe, turned one screw and in less than 90 seconds handed a bill to the owner for $25,000. When asked how it was possible to charge $25,000 to turn one screw, the engineer replied, "Oh, it's only $1.00 to turn the screw. It's $24,999 to know which screw to turn!"

"IT DOESN'T TAKE MUCH TO MAKE US HAPPY!"
SPEED LIMIT 55

XXVIII
In Closing

If you feel connected with the thinking described in these pages, call 866-458-4514 and let's set up a time to talk.—John Borzellino

"There was never a genius
without a tincture of insanity."
Aristotle